Astrology in the 21st Century

Edu Petriat

While every precaution has been taken in the preparation of this book, the publisher assumes no responsibility for errors or omissions, or for damages resulting from the use of the information contained herein.

ASTROLOGY FOR THE 21ST CENTURY

First edition. May 25, 2024.

ISBN: 979-8224589869

Written by Edu Petriati.

Table of Contents

Translation from '*La Astrologia en el Siglo XXI*'
www.elnuevocamino.com[1]

Acknowledgements

My sincere and eternal thanks go to my teacher and guide on the subject of astrology, Luis Cleve, who is sadly no longer with us and I wish to offer my appreciation to Luis Montenegro for using his great talent and creativity in the cover design, making sure that it fully reflects the concept of the book.

Introduction

The aim of this book is to prompt consideration and discussion on topics related to astrology in this modern era, marked by immense advances in science and technology, and the growing acceptance of their importance in the global consciousness. We only have to look back some 20 years into the past to realize how much our lives have changed by technology. Owing to almost instant access to information, many previously specialized topics have become common knowledge.

Thus, it is inevitable that our understanding of astrology has changed, as new scientific discoveries have prompted revision of some of its concepts, without changing its essence or undermining the value of ancestral knowledge. While certain things do not change over time, today's technology opens the possibility of achieving a better understanding of aspects that once could only be a matter of belief, faith, or acceptance.

We live in an important period in human history, as we are finally able to shed light on some previously inexplicable phenomena, with the ultimate aim of better understanding the reason behind them and the purpose of things. This does not change the wonderful and immense magnitude of the essence of our existence, but it provides the opportunity to move on to another reality, to another level of understanding of the process of evolution.

Certain discussions presented in this book may sound obvious to those with previous astrological knowledge. Still, such individuals will benefit from some technological aspects that may or may not converge with the astrological aspects. In presenting this manuscript in this manner, the aim is not to force these concepts into a cohesive unit, but to determine what aspects of astrology can pass the rigorous scientific analysis in order to be able to enunciate them.

The goal of this analysis is to understand how the energy generated by the planets in relation to our natal chart affects our personal characteristics and our lives. Although each astrologer knows that it is possible to measure the strength of a transit, planet, and aspect, it is not easy to explain how this energy reaches us and materializes in our psyche and our body (1).

We know that everything in the world is interconnected (the famous butterfly effect), but we often struggle to understand the causes of phenomena and their underlying mechanisms.

For a long time, it was a common knowledge that radio and TV content was transmit via a signal, which these devices receive and transform into something that our senses can capture and process. Yet, we rarely stop to consider that these signals are constantly passing through our body and we do not even realize it. If we had a wave display device, it would have shown us that we were immersed in a soup of frequencies.

If 20 years ago someone mentioned the word "Wi-Fi" no one would know what this term meant. Yet, today, we are all using technology dependent on Wi-Fi, which surrounds us and passes through our bodies 24 hours a day. If we could see our environment in its entirety, we would realize that we are immersed in a very thick stew. The movie "The Matrix," which was presented as science fiction, provided a glimpse into this 'parallel reality', which is rapidly being realized. Indeed, we are now fully aware that there are certain aspects of our reality that we do not see.

There are signal inhibitors, which can block a house, a building, an area of the city so that the devices do not work (2). These devices do not eliminate the presence of these signals; they merely make them unintelligible to the devices that have to receive them. Interesting, right?

Just as there are frequencies generated by devices made by human beings, certain frequencies and electromagnetic radiation exist in our environment, such as those characterizing ultraviolet rays, X-rays, gamma rays, etc. Currently, there are satellites inside and outside the Earth's atmosphere that measure radiation coming from the Sun and from outer space. When the so-called solar storms occur, different types of energies are release, affecting the Earth. Depending on the intensity of this energy is possible the prediction of auroras borealis among other things.

In addition, we know the effects of Moon's gravity on tides on Earth, but not only, since it can also affect our mood and even agriculture. Thus, it is logical to ponder on the effects of other celestial bodies in each one of us.

Applying this reasoning to astrology, it is valid to ask if there is a way to evaluate the specific weight of a given planetary transit through their measurement by the effect it produces. We will try to investigate about this topic in this book.

To understand if there is a way to modify the energy that we are receiving, we should first examine how it makes its way to us. Just as astrology comes from antiquity, also several methods based on frequency for improving the physical and mental state of people are present today. Hence, we need to consider if there are mechanisms or practices within our reach today that can vary the intensity or energy of the aspects under certain planetary transits.

We will try to analyze these points and see if today, with the existing information, we can better understand and expand our knowledge of the functioning of the universe, astrology, and the human beings.

Some important references on astrology:

- Astrology is more than 3000 years old. For a long time, the planets were representing gods, and each on them having certain characteristics.

- The Babylonians were aware of the transit of Jupiter 1000 years before the telescope was invented (3).

- The first natal charts based on the month in which a person was born date to 1300 BC.

- Astrology was use to anticipate important events and for knowing the possible destinies of those born.

- Given the restrictions that Catholic Church imposed on the study of the human body, astrology use in relation to the human body arrived in Europe from the Middle East around 1400 AD, even though it was already an ancient practice in the east and in Egypt in particular.

- One of the most famous publications in English language related to astrology and medicine is Richard Saunders' *The Astrological Judgment and Practice of Physick* (4), first published in 1677 and is still in circulation. During his 30 years of medical practice, Saunders paid close attention to the relationship between astrological issues and diseases.

- Paracelsus (5), whose real name was Theophrastus Phillippus Aureolus Bombastus von Hohenheim, lived from the late 1400s to the mid-1500s in what is now Switzerland. He was a renowned physician and astrologer, who used the hermetic principles in his profession. He is known for his contribution to the study of magnetism and its effects on human body.

- Dane Rudhyar (6), whose real name is Daniel Chenneviere, was born in France, where he lived from the late 1800s to 1985. He was a musician, composer, and astrologer, and was the first to examine the psychological aspects of astrology. Rudhyar gave rise to the birth of "astrological psychology." Rudhyar took into account the developments of the Swiss psychologist Carl Jung, and his work consisted of synthesizing that knowledge within astrology.

It is interesting that Chenneviere used the pseudonym Rudhyar, which derives from the god Rudra (Sanskrit), known as the Destroyer and Regenerator.

- Uranus was discovered in 1781, Neptune in 1846, and Pluto in 1930; each of these planets is associated with a certain important period and has affected the social, political, and technological events in the world.

- Chiron, a comet with an erratic trajectory discovered in 1977, is the last one considered in the natal chart called the "wound healer."

- The widespread use of personal computers that started in the late 1970s prompted the development of systems for the construction of natal charts and other functions. Advancements in this field continue, benefitting further from many online sources.

This brief historical review has the intention to highlight how we got to where we are today, considering some of the important steps in the evolution of astrological knowledge, and how this knowledge covers more aspects than a simple analysis aimed at predicting the future.

Today depends on yesterday, and tomorrow is conditioned by today

In the same way that astrology evolved (like any other science) from its inception until now, it has been expanding its reach without losing anything of its original concepts. Rather, the focus has been on perfecting it and expanding its scope by including new areas. The first astrologers were priests that served under the orders of rulers who were in power. This practice has survived to this day, as exemplified by the famous astrologer who advised President Regan in the 1980s (7). In addition, astrology had its presence in the Catholic Church (several Popes of antiquity were astrologers), scientists and doctors, and other individuals with an important place in history, such as Benjamin Franklin, one of the promoters of the independence of the United States.

We arrived today after going through an evolutionary process, where it may be possible a qualitative jump based on all the technology and information available. Just as an example, in the professional field of biology, at the beginning of the 20th century, the idea was that there was nothing more to discover, as we knew already how the human body works. Yet, it all changed due to the discovery of DNA, stem cells, and the new branch of epigenetics (8).

With the current technological advances, it is possible that astrology will evolve through new studies and discoveries. Given the changes that have taken place in all scientific fields, would anyone dare to say that everything has been discover or that astrology cannot advance further?

In biology, the cell nucleus was for a long time considered its 'brain.' Yet, continued research has disproved this view, given that if the nucleus is extracted from the cell, the cell continues to live, with the only limitation that it cannot reproduced. It is logical to think that a living being cannot remain alive if its main processing parts, such as the brain, is remove.

This is just a simple example of something that was a common accepted belief, was refute by new discoveries.

The important thing is not to discard or rethink everything regarding astrology, but to take the existing knowledge and deepen the study with all available means, aiming to confirm or refute the new findings, or make the necessary adjustments to existing concepts. Everything is in the state of constant motion.

Another concept that can be misinterpreted is that we are not victims of the stars and our natal charts. In the antiquity, they had that vision and, in some way, it made it to our days.

For example, long time ago, in some Arab countries, infants born under an eclipse were kill just to spare them a life of suffering. Yet, Pope John Paul II was born under an eclipse (and died under an eclipse). Depending on which side of his life you want to see, he had a complicated or interesting life, but it was full and meaningful. Those that are born under an eclipse undoubtedly face burdens and we must see how these will affect their lives, but certainly not a reason to be extinguish at birth.

Owing to the evolution in the field of astrology, and thanks to the work conducted by Rudhyar, psychological knowledge was include into the analysis of natal charts. On the other hand, great advances made in natural sciences, such as biology, physics, and quantum mechanics, which could potentially have meaningful impact on astrology.

At present time, we cannot refer to the astrological aspects in the same way that it was done 500 years ago, especially in the Western world. Today, many people are trying to find ways to overcome their limitations and to evolve—aspirations that were reserved only for elite in the Middle Ages. Throughout most of the human history, majority of the population was merely trying to survive, focusing on food, shelter or security, rather than self-fulfillment and evolution.

On the evolutionary scale of human development, we have made a significant progress, as most of us have solved the issues related to subsistence (home, food, health, education). Although poverty is still an issue in many parts of the world, in general, we can say that we are at a much greater evolutionary level than ever before.

As in life, as in astrology, it is worth highlighting the comparison that, if the son of the king and the son of the beggar are born in the same town at the same time, they will have the same natal chart, but the transits they will have during their life, will affect them differently, as everything is relative. The same can be mention of a person who is on an evolutionary path relative to someone who merely transits through life, not conscious of life purpose. The natal chart provides the core characteristics, but the person and its environment will determine how these will interact through life. The planetary transits will affect differently a person with a certain degree of evolution to someone that considers itself a victim of consequences.

Dr. Oskar Adler already spoke of the two possible states of evolution for each planet in the natal chart, which could be represented (characteristics) in the evolutionary aspect of their energies, or in the aspect of their low frequencies.

After providing this brief summary, outlining what this work is about and delineating information that has existed for a long time, in the next section; we will explore the current knowledge and see what adaptations to astrology are possible. Everything is in constant flow, nothing is static, and astrology fits into this pattern.

Let us start with the understanding of the human body, and its relation to astrology.

The Human Body

In astrology, each part of the human body is recognize by a sign. Thus, the head is represented by Aries and the process continues until we reach the feet, associated with Pisces, with the other signs distributed in a downward direction from the head downwards.

With regard to the birth chart and the human body, the following can be said:

- The zodiacal signs govern the anatomy (9).
- The planets govern physiology (10).
- The houses of the natal chart are the points of expression and causes of planetary actions.

In relation to health, astrology considers House VI and that in opposition, House XII. House VI relates to the organs and the physical body, and House XII carries the mental theme.

Depending on the signs, planets present in the natal chart and their aspects, that's how the energies/frequencies of the planets reflect in the different parts of the body.

As mentioned above, the sign of the house in the natal chart determines the preponderant part of the body taken into account in astrology.

For example, we can say that, if House VI is in Pisces with bad aspects, it can indicate problems with the feet, which would manifest through different ailments or discomforts. That is define as a natal aspect in the same way as any hereditary characteristic.

The Moon exerts a significant effect on us, mainly our mental states, regardless of whether we realize it or not. Saying "I am moody" has an important astrological connotation. The Moon takes around 28 days to transit our natal chart and, during that period, it will travel through the 12 houses and activate all possible aspects with each home planet. When certain aspects are given, these will generate energies that can influence our moods. Hence, it is not an "urban legend" that emotions run high during full moon, when people are generally more exalted, and more violent events may occur.

The Moon primarily affects our psychic part and, depending on other aspects, it may or may not affect the normal functioning of our organism.

The Arabs were very aware of the lunar cycles and defined what is called "lunar mansions." The timing of the Moon's entry in each sign and its transit through it is highly important. The cycle begins when the Moon enters Aries and going through each "mansion" until it completes the cycle. As each mansion has specific characteristics, depending on which one is active, a recommendation to do or avoid certain actions is advice.

Examined from the point of view of health, depending on in which mansion the Moon is located, certain tests or medical procedures would be favorable to carry out or avoid. Of course, we are talking about something that can be schedule.

For example, when the Moon enters Aries—, which corresponds, to mansions 1, 2 and 3—it is recommended to avoid any type of treatment or study that involves the head (Aries), such as surgeries, dental treatments, ophthalmological measurements, and others. More information found in the reference. (11)

It is known that human body is composed of more than 70% water, our cells work with electricity (very low voltage), and that water is an excellent conductor of electricity. We can use our fingers on the screens of smartphones, tablets, computers and other capacitive devices because, through our body (mainly the fingers in this case), by producing an interference in the electric current of the screen. While there are already more than 6 different systems, some of which work with pressure (and other methods are still being investigated), the so-called capacitive is the one that uses our voltage interference to activate the area that is touched on the screen (12).

Dr. Jerry Tennant is a licensed physician practicing in Dallas, Texas. In addition to being on the board of the Arizona Homeopathic Medicine organization licensed by the Pastoral Medical Association, Dr. Tennant has conducted studies of how electric current works in the human body, as well as what it means when this process is disrupted. His work allows us to understand better the construction of the human body as well as it functions (13).

However, rather than delving into medical issues, the aim of this discussion is to present information that we can use in our conclusions, always bearing in mind that everything is interconnected.

Through his studies, Dr. Tennant demonstrated the following:

Energy is produce in the mitochondria in our cells that act as rechargeable batteries where ADP (adenosine diphosphate) without charge is transformed into ATP (adenosine triphosphate) loaded through a process called Krebs Cycle. A molecule of fat normally produces 48 ATPs, but it will produce only 2 ATPs if there is a lack of oxygen, and as a consequence, one feels tired and listless.

The ATP is the rechargeable battery used in enzymatic functions. We must also bear in mind that, in a low oxygen environment (in cells), the microbes that are in the body wake up and begin to produce digestive enzymes that feed on nearby cells. Mycotoxins can affect other parts of the body once they enter the circulatory system. This occurs at any time that the voltage in the cell is low.

The effects of low flow of electricity includes:

1) Chronic pain

2) Lack of oxygen
3) Metabolic inefficiency
4) Growth of viruses, bacteria, yeast, and fungi

As can be seen, imbalance in the electrical charge of each cell can lead to an imbalance, causing transient problems or chronic diseases, but the most important thing to highlight at this point are the causes that can determine this electrical change in the cells.

According to the available evidence, certain aspects between planets and houses in particular can generate certain mental disorders, which put the patient in a state not aligned with the surrounding reality. This could be define as a change in the "rational programs" of the person. In the case of Dr. Tennant's study, it has more to do with the physical apparatus and organic functioning of the human body.

If we understand how the human body works, we can appreciate how a medicine works. Any medication that we take, either pharmacological or natural, works in the body with the objective of balancing a part that is malfunctioning due to some imbalance. As mentioned in relation to the process of ATP generation, if the corresponding energy is not generated because of a malfunctioning, this leads to illness and a need to see the doctor. The medication that is supplied will, through chemical processes in the body, interfere with the malfunction and bring our body to its normal state.

In other words, medication is a tool that acts on a certain malfunction in the body in order to restore balance. This works in a way similar to our daily interactions in our home or with our things. We use soaps and innumerable amounts of cleaning fluids on a daily basis, which produce a chemical reaction that removes dirt from our clothes, pots, floors, and so on.

There are hundreds of thousands of cleaning products for the home, in the same way that there are hundreds of thousands of medicines on the market, all work base on chemical reactions. The operating mechanisms are similar, but the complexity of their action depends on the components involved.

There is the mechanical part of our body and the logical part (integrated with the mechanical one) which we can define as rational programs, discussed in detail in the reference (14). For now, we will focus on the mechanical aspects of our body.

Summary of this section

Someone at some point will have heard or read the phrase, "as above, so below, as below, so above," or another with a religious connotation, "on earth as it is in heaven," which ultimately expresses the same notion.

Both the functioning of a cell and the functioning of the human body work under the same basic principles. After all, the human body is composed of trillions of cells, with more or less the same components (15).

The natal chart gives us a definition of the composition of the human body and the physical characteristics from the head to the feet. In the natal chart, you can identify the most vulnerable parts of the body in relation to the signs, planets, and their aspects.

Human beings are not exempt from the influence of the energy of the Moon, which also affects the tides, agriculture, the embryonic processes, and others. Neither is the Moon an exception, since the other planets have their "type of energy," which influences both our psychic and physical parts. The integration of psychology within astrology by Rudhyar based on the studies of Carl Jung clearly demonstrates these influences.

We know that Saturn is a "heavy energy" planet, which generates restrictive energies, whereas Jupiter generates expansive energies. Considering this when you want to follow some type of diet to lose weight, for example, it is important, as the transits of both Saturn and Jupiter may influence your success.

If you try to lose weight during a transit of conjunction, sextile, or trine of Jupiter with the Sun, Moon or Venus, you will not get good results. During those periods, the individual will have more appetite, and will be more attracted to sweets and other things that make it difficult to lose weight. Conversely, a transit of Saturn can help in that aspect, beyond the other things that can happen as "collateral damage", given the restrictive energy in the environment. This observation should be taken only as a reference, since we are not conducting analysis of each transit or planet. The natal chart is personal, like the transits, and each person has to be analyze base on its personal natal char to obtain an effective diagnosis.

This example merely aims to emphasize existence of a direct relationship among the birth chart, the transits, the planets, and the human body. In the same way that the Moon can affect our state of mind, which is ultimately nothing more than energy that activates certain programs in our body, the planets in the Solar System, without a doubt, also exert their influence on the functioning of our body and our psyche, as it does with the earth and the environment.

Thinking of our body and our health, the old Latin motto "Mens sana in corpore sano" (healthy mind, healthy body) contains all the possible wisdom. May this simple sentence tell us that, if we are mentally balanced, centered, and aligned within ourselves, our body will be less exposed to the vagaries of our environment (including the celestial bodies) and we will maintain our body balance and in good health.

When a person is been described as somewhat "heavy" or "dense," are we indirectly talking about the energies and frequencies that this person generates? Conversely, is a "being of light," as it may be called; is it referring to someone that is vibrating at a very high frequency?

Let's continue with the topic of frequencies and see if this allows us to delve more deeply into how our body works, which should resemble the workings of the Universe, as expressed in the familiar saying "as above, so below."

Vibrations, Sounds, and Frequencies

To understand frequencies, as energies that may or may not materialize, one must start from a scientific definition stating that **the degree of solidity of an entity is determine by its state of vibration.**

According to the quantum physics postulates, everything in the universe is composed of particles, and particles are compose by atoms. That is what we learned in general education. However, while these elements will exist in the form of atoms, molecules, or compounds, these can be further decompose in subatomic particles, such as electrons, protons, neutrons, and further still to entities that only exist given their vibrational state. Thus, the degree of vibration will determine the degree of "solidity" with which the element is identified or recognized. From the maximum to the minimum level. There is an infinite number of vibratory ranges.

Quantum physicists have discovered that the so-called subatomic particles are not particles per se, but forms of pure vibratory energy characterized by the quantum probabilities under which they can manifest themselves, in different and varied forms.

An experiment carried out by Thomas Yung in 1801 called the "Double-Slit Experiment" (16) and its subsequent investigations and modifications allow us to appreciate that things are not really fixed or predetermined, but that we have significant influence over them. The simple fact of observation, intention, and expectation has an influence on the subject.

The original experiment worked by passing photon's beam through a double grid and seeing how it registered on a photographic film. The researchers were surprised to see that, rather than a figure following the shape of the slit, they observed a waveform on the photographic film.

Repeating the experiment, but this time placing an apparatus to observe what changes were taking place when the photon beam passed through the slit, they found that the result was different to the first one, and the film reflected the slit format. That was the expected result the first time.

In short, by "observing" how the experiment worked, the result changed. For more detail of the experiment, please refer to the reference.

Considering the results of this experiment and the existing knowledge of frequencies and vibrations, we can say the following:

1. A particle (which is something physical) can also behave like a wave (frequency)

2. Everything in the universe works based of frequencies that vary across an infinite range (17)

3. The frequency range determines whether we can register something or not with our senses

4. Both human beings and everything around us, including the planets, vibrates and emanates certain frequency

In sum, besides that everything is vibration, also how hard can be to understand, there is no pre-determinism. The observer can change the outcome of things.

The experiment done, prove that the observer can change the result of something by the mere fact of "observing." This clearly tells us that there is a communication and exchange of energy between the observer and what is been observed. When you observe something, you are not necessarily looking to change the result, but the fact of observing still has consequences.

Let us now ponder on the fact that, when "intention" is add to an observation, consequently, the result may vary significantly, since the simple energy interacting in the observation, is now compound by the energy of the intention. The aforementioned interaction shows that our thoughts generate a vibration or wave, which manifests itself in the physical plane, generating a result. In other words, although thought is something that we do not see (but it could be measure), it is "materialized" through a physical change. This fact clarifies the relationship between the "energy" plane (high vibrational density) and the "physical" plane (low vibrational density).

Based on the aforementioned experiment and in relation to astrology, it would reasonable to consider **the natal chart as "the grid," the planets as the "observers," and us as the "result" of the observation.**

Sound is a mechanical wave. For example, we know that a very loud sound at a certain frequency can produce a high vibration in objects, which can be broken depending on their composition.

As an additional comment on the matter, as an example of resonant frequency, the changing of the pace of a regiment of soldiers crossing a bridge, can already give an idea of the meaning this has. The question is how many bridges fell before they learn that they fell, not because of bad construction, but because the frequency produced by the soldiers marching in unison coincided with the natural vibration frequency of the bridge, causing its structure to "disarticulate."

Here, we should pause to consider the fact that sound (which is not solid matter) could break something that it is consider solid. The explanation is simple, as everything in the Universe is composed of the same essence, albeit at different vibratory level, which gives different entities their "consistency."

The frequency range that humans can hear as audible sound ranges from 20 vibrations per second (cycles or Hertz, Hz) to 20,000 vibrations per second. The audible range will depend on the age and condition of the person's hearing.

Electricity and heat vibrate between billion and trillion vibrations per second. The spectrum of colors visible to the human eye vibrates at five hundred billion per second. In the same way, we can continue upwards and we find the infrared, ultraviolet rays until we reach the X-rays, which vibrate at two trillion per second.

Some colors and their wave frequencies:

Color Frequency Wavelength
Violet 668–789 THz 380–450 nm
Blue 606–668 450–495
Green 526–606 495–570
Yellow 508–526 570–599

We know that there are more levels, but we presently do not have devices capable of measuring them.

Let's keep the thought that it cannot be said that something "does not exist" simply because we do not have the technical capacity to measure it.

Who can affirm today that there will not be new discoveries that could expand our knowledge of how things work? Our history teaches us that many "scientific facts" were later prove untrue, as shown in the example of biology in the early 1900s.

At this point, I will share a short story from my student life that relates to aspects that one usually does not consider and interfere with in our surroundings at every moment. When I studied computer science, I had several highly educated teachers that had interesting jobs in addition to teaching. For example, one was a consultant for JPL (Jet Propulsion Laboratory under NASA), while another was a researcher at CALTECH.

In a class explaining how we need to be careful when conducting analyses on variables that could affect a result, our professor shared his experience working on a military project. They had developed a system for automatic missile defense response, which had to be activated when some variation in the atmospheric temperature was detected (in theory, the change would be produced by a missile coming from that direction).

The system was in test and simulation stage, as a part of which, they were collecting information and making the necessary corrections.

Certain night, the system activated automatically and simulated the activation of missile interception protocol. The system received information from geostationary satellites in the atmosphere and other ground devices. The first thing they thought was that they had some problem in the program or that some control device was malfunctioning.

What they discovered after a more detailed analysis was that, during the full moon, the temperature of the Earth's atmosphere increased sufficiently to trigger the launch signal. That variable was not consider.

Although it may seem that this event has nothing to do with astrology, it shows how changes in our environment can affect us. Heat is a consequence of an increase in the variation of vibration range and, in this particular case; the Moon was responsible for this change. The changes that Moon produces in the environment, which is not only heat as mentioned, has consequences in us, and they could be measure. The same could happen with the other celestial bodies.

Today, we know that the cells in the human body vibrate in the 50−1500 Hz range, corresponding to the wavelengths in the 6200−7000 Å. The viruses that can produce diseases vibrate in the wavelength range below 5500 Å. For example, the Koch's bacillus of tuberculosis vibrates at 5500 Å and the cancer vibrates at 4000 Å. At this point, it is worth noting that a low level of vibration in cells represents a disease.

In the link of the reference there is a very detailed explanation of what we are talking about by and explanation of Daniel Taroppio, who participated in the framework of the Congress "Science, Psychology and Spirituality" attended by Stanislav Grof and Humberto Maturana (18).

Carl Sagan in his famous television series Cosmos made the demonstration of filling a test tube the size of a person with the exact proportion of water and other elements that make up the human body. He applied an electric charge (as noted previously, the human body works based on that same principle), and the liquid in the test tube did not change. Having the same material composition and charging them with an electric charge, nothing happen.

Our bodies are composed from the skeleton (the hardest) to tears (the softest) with the same proportion of elements as the test tube, but we are an extremely complex system involving an immense quantity of mechanisms that work based on chemical reactions and electricity. While there are many things that we still do not know about the human body today, let us continue our analysis of the things we do know.

There are laws that can exceed our understanding, because, with the information available today, we can affirm that EVERYTHING is in continuous vibration, but physical laws that we still do not understand, keep everything within its form, proportion, and content.

Japanese researcher Masuro Emoto, who was criticize in scientific circles for the methods he used, demonstrated that the water molecule could change depending on the frequency to which it is exposed. He used music of various types and managed to photograph the different forms that the water particle took depending on the type of music to which it was exposed. Emoto's work was the precursor of this type of analysis, but today many musicians, technicians, and investigators are carrying out experiments to study the reaction of water when exposed to different frequencies (19). The progress in this line of research has led to the emergence of a new scientific field—Cymatics (20).

The fact is that we are composed of more than 70% of water, and all the frequencies (both local and foreign) that surround us and pass through our body affect us at every moment. It would be reasonable to think that this may have some impact on our physical and mental functioning.

If we focus on the functioning of our brain, we know that it produces different types of brainwaves as the following:

- Beta waves have a frequency of 15–40 Hz, and are wide and fast. They have a greater presence when the person is fully awake. The "beta state" is the common state of everyday life and can be associated with common thoughts, work, and problem solving.

- Alpha waves oscillate at 9–14 Hz, and are thus broader and slower than beta waves. They usually manifest when the person is in a state of relaxation, usually while physically at rest. These waves can be produced consciously when meditating. The "alpha state" is usually associated with relaxation, super learning, increased intuition, and overcoming stress.

- Theta waves are even wider and move even slower than the previous ones, at 5–8 Hz. These waves are emitted by the brain when the person is in a state of deep meditation, or just before crossing the threshold of sleep, just after awakening, or moments before sleep. They can also occur in an almost unconscious imaginative free state that occurs when we "daydream." The "theta state" is often associated with creativity and states conducive to healing.

- Delta waves have the greatest amplitude and are the slowest, at 0.1–4 Hz. Their frequency never reaches zero since the living brain never stops working. These brainwaves are present while we are in "the deepest sleep state." The "delta state" relates to the famous growth hormone, which is responsible for the recovery of health and cell repair needed to combat aging of the body. Due to this property, the "delta state" is also associated with the healing and regeneration of tissues.

- Gamma waves, recently discovered by neuroscience, are the fastest, since their frequency ranges from 40 to 100 Hz. These are not associated with everyday thoughts, although they relate to a great mental activity that can include flashes of brilliance and sudden experiences of perception/intuition, as well as moments of extreme attention, concentration, and lucidity.

Given the above, it is evident that the state of a person can be define at every moment by measuring the frequency at which its brain is working. Any brain state could change at any time irrespective of whether the person is awake or asleep. There are different techniques or procedures available today that can achieve that.

When one wakes up "moody," without any apparent reason and this mood goes away after a little while, we can use astrology to determine what aspect of the Moon could be working during that period. One can agree that the brain was affect by certain frequency coming from the combination of a **natal chart/Moon** transit aspect, altering the brain frequency, until the effect of the transit passes.

In the same way that the brain was "affected" by a certain wave or frequency, we can influence it by generating other frequencies that could neutralize the imbalances produced by a given planetary transit.

Certain cells can be develop from stem cells, and can take certain characteristics based on their environment. The environment influence has an important effect in cells as for human beings. Taken this into account, we can see how an external influence such as binaural sounds, can produce changes in the frequency ranges of the brain, and therefore produce changes in our mood and perception of our environment.

Binaural sounds are produced by devices similar to portable music player (21), used with headphones and special glasses, which produce sounds and lights of different frequencies depending on the desired results the person is looking to achieve. The glasses generate flashes of light between the red and green color, which twinkle in the same wave as the sound heard in the headphones.

There is a wide range of programs aimed at different mental states. For example, there are different relaxation programs, others to increase creativity, meditation, and so on.

These systems work by direct induction of sound and light, which can produce a change in the brainwave state. Their use does not create addiction or have side effects on a normal functioning brain.

Similar results could be achieve naturally through a process of meditation and similar practices. Still, under an active "complicated" astrological transit, concentration can be more difficult, or there could be other distractions that would make a task at other moments easily or enjoyable, hard to achieve.

It is clear that we are a product of our environment captured by our senses. However, even though we are not aware of their influence, the planetary transits can affect us, and should thus be consider part of "our environment". These transits are personal and interact with our natal chart. Our environment directly influences the functioning of our brain and, therefore, all our mental and physical actions and reactions.

It is worth noting that the same transit will not affect everyone equally, since there is a large number of personal variables to consider in each case. Just recalling what was mention about the Moon and the missiles, for better evaluation and good results, all variables have to be considerate.

Summary of this section

In this section, we discussed the nature of the world around us and our ability to change our environment simply by interacting or observing. Such changes may not be perceptible, but can be measure with the right device.

The human body is a very complex cellular machine comprised of interrelated organs that, in its natural development, starting taking shape from the moment of fertilization when the ovule was divided into 2 cells, then 4, then 8, until the full organism was formed. Not only is it composed of mechanical parts, it also has a logical processing center integrated with the physical, which also began to form from the moment of conception. This processing, which works based on certain frequencies and electrical impulses, activates certain parts of the body, which will materialize in sounds and actions that will interact both with the environment and within the body itself.

There is a third component, which is known as the spiritual, but that is not addressed here, and it is left for the experts on that subject. Astrology touches upon the concepts of higher beliefs and their development, but it is not involve with the different religions and/or belief systems. Astrology focuses on the analysis of a person beyond the religion, sex, or present beliefs system. No discrimination or categorization is part of the analysis.

It is very important to understand that the path that each person follows, beyond the natal chart, is govern by the attitudes or responses to the different situations the person encounters in the daily life. What we have to be aware and always present is that the behavior and, in particular, the mood that at any moment is generate, can be modify or manage.

In defining the state of mind as a certain frequency range the human body is generating, we must not lose sight of the fact that this affects both our environment and the internal parts of the body.

When the person is going through a "pessimistic" period, for example, they see everything as wrong, and look for problems in everything, even when there is none. If this attitude persists, it is likely that, as a result, the immune system will be negative affected.

Beyond the effects of the cause of that particular state of mind, weakened immune system would make it more likely for different agents to damage our health. As described in the section on the human body, when the oxygen (vibration) level in the cell is low, the bacteria, fungi, and other species that are already present in the body or could come from the outside begin to feed on the healthy cells, and inevitably adversely affect our health and wellbeing.

Astrology allows us to determine the periods where the different energies are going to have a significant impact on the person, and this information allows preparing physically and mentally in advance. What is the difference between this and going out with an umbrella if you know that it is going to rain?

To live a healthy life, both our physical and mental functioning must work within certain frequency ranges, as this is the key to a balanced life. There will be good and bad periods, but staying "centered" beyond the cycle that is being traveled, is the key to the evolutionary process.

In the section that follows, we will see how, since ancient times, techniques based on sounds were use to modify the energetic and/or vibratory imbalances in the human body, and how this practice made it to present time.

Sonic Healing in Antiquity and Today

From the macrocosm to the microcosm, we exist and live in a sea of sounds and frequencies that can be mathematically describe as harmonic relationships.

Geneticists have deciphered the musical expression of our DNA; NASA has captured the sounds of all planets, including the sound of black holes; and in November 2014, the Rosetta probe of the European Space Agency recorded the sound of a comet (22).

Sound travels approximately four times faster through water than through air. Given the percentage of water in our bodies, it is apparent that the human body rapidly responds to sounds / frequencies to which it is exposed.

At present, environmental pollution (23) has reached unprecedented levels. Within all the polluting factors, we need to consider the ambient or background noise. The main consequences of being expose to noise pollution include the interference in communication, hearing disorders, sleep disturbance, stress, and all its consequences. We are so used to noise in our daily lives, that we do not realize the aggression we receive from the sounds produced by everything around us. When we are in a peaceful and silent place, that is when we feel a different sensation and we place ourselves in another time/space relationship. Silence is like applying the brake to the speed produced by our daily routine.

Every sound that surrounds us is being perceive by our senses depending on the frequency it produces. There are natural sounds, such as rain, running water, wind rustling the leaves of trees, birds, and other elements that vibrate at frequencies to which we are attune. On the other hand, noises such as those produced by engines, machinery, screams, and many others of the kind, are aggressive to our senses. For this reason, for someone who lives in the middle of nature and is accustomed to natural noises, the level of noise in a city could cause a shock. Those of us, who are "adapted" to these noises due to living in such environments for a long time, will only notice noises that "exceed" the "normal" level of the city.

It is common to lose the perspective on things, and makes us forget that we are beings with a construction designed for a life in an environment consistent with our organic composition, which requires maintaining a healthy mental and physical balance. Even though we are "adaptable" beings, each adaptation to a hostile environment, has a burden and a price to pay, it is not free.

Just seeing how people react in general when they are heading off for a long holiday or vacation or even celebrating that is "Friday" gives us an idea of our constant need to "escape" from the daily imbalances produced by the routine of our busy environment. One could say without exaggeration that this way of life is the main reason behind so many mental illnesses, causing people to turn to psychologists, psychiatrists, or medicines to calm anxiety, depression, and other ailments, caused primarily by the deviation from the natural way of living and cost for adaptation to an hostile environment.

Returning to the issue of noise pollution and the effect it produces on human beings, having discussed frequencies and sounds, we can see that the well-known "environmental contamination by noise" is something that affects us both psychically and physically. The purpose of this analysis is to see how sounds could be used to balance both our psychic and physical elements.

Since ancient times, "healing" frequencies have been use for helping restore the balance in both body and mind. As far as we know today, in those days, the degree of noise pollution that we have today did not exist, but there were always energy deviations in people, represented by different disorders and diseases.

Without losing sight of astrology and the influences related to our natal chart and planetary transits, we continue the analysis on what type of energies are present under certain aspects and the effects that these could have. The better we can interpret the lower energies in play, the better we can identify what frequencies to use trying to counteract their temporal effects.

At this point, it is important to highlight that the aim of this method is not to "avoid or cheat" in the natural evolutionary process of the person. Rather, the goal is to provide those who are in the pursuit of their evolution with tools that can help them move forward at critical moments. The mere fact that a person is considering the options available to support a difficult period in life, which could have been anticipated by astrology, this hints that the person is on the right track in the evolutionary process.

There are techniques that can be adopt for redressing both physical ailments and mental imbalances, but these have to be apply during certain periods and they should be accompanie by certain changes in personal habits. No significant changes can be expect just by being under the influence of a given transit and the use of a temporary technique for support. Still, these must be just the "triggers" of the actions that will follow, along with the change in the person's mental attitude.

In critical periods, we tend to analyze the situation and all the elements that are relevant for that situation, without paying much attention to the history or previous cycles. A very important aspect to understand is that, everything that happens at a certain moment will be condition by past events and actions. As it is commonly said, "what made you sick was not the last drink, but every drink you had before that."

Similarly, during a medical checkup, after examining the test results, the doctor can advise the patient to exercise more, stop eating fats or sugars, or make other lifestyle changes. The same applies in astrology, as it provides the diagnosis, and this is just that. It will be up to the individual to make the necessary changes or adjustments in order to move forward and prevent being stuck in life at certain moment in time, which will prevent growth and evolution. Evolution is achieve by living life in harmony. The birth chart, the transits, and progressions will give a diagnosis, and could be pointing to one of the various forms of therapies, depending on the case, and some could include sound therapy. However, they will only work to a certain extent, as they usually need to be accompany by changes in lifestyle and/or attitude.

One of the currently available alternatives is "psionic medicine" that can determine, by using radiesthesia faculties, causes of the imbalance in the dynamic vital forces behind disorders and diseases (24).

Dr. Peter Guy Manners (25), British scientist who created the Cymatic Instrument that projects sounds into the body for healing, describes this phenomenon of frequency resonance in this way: "A healthy organ will have its molecules working together in a harmonious relationship with each other and they will all be of the same pattern. If different sound patterns enter the organ, the harmonious relationship could be altered ... they can establish their disharmonic pattern in the organ, the bone tissue, etc., and this is what we call disease. Therefore, if a treatment contains a pattern of harmonic frequency that will strengthen the organs, the vibrations of the intruders will be neutralize, and the correct pattern for that organ will be restored. This should be a healing reaction."

Dr. Alfred Tomatis (26)—internationally renowned otolaryngologist, psychologist, researcher, and inventor—spent around 50 years studying the hearing and its special function. In his view, hearing is the most important of our five senses because the hearing take control of the state of balance, rhythm, and movement of the body. They also coordinate and connect with the nervous system.

Through the marrow, the auditory nerve connects with the muscles of the body. Therefore, the muscle tone, balance, flexibility, and even the vision are affected by sounds. Moreover, the inner ear is connect to the larynx, then to other organs, such as the heart, lungs, stomach, liver, bladder, kidneys, and small and large intestines.

Tomatis considers that the most frequent sounds, corresponding to frequencies above 3000 Hz, can activate the brain and affect our cognitive functioning, thus interfering with a person's thinking, spatial perception, and memory. He also believes that listening to high-frequency sounds increases concentration and attention.

In 2002, while working in the Department of Chemistry at UCLA (University of California, Los Angeles), Professor James Gimzewski (27) and Andrew Pelling discovered cellular sounds, while observing certain cells that oscillated with audible frequencies within the nanoscale. This gave rise to "Sonocytology" (28)—the study of the sounds generated by different cells—which is a completely new field of research.

The microscope use to determine the atomic force (AFM) invented in 1986 by Binnig, Quate and Gerber, and since then it has become an incredibly useful tool in physics, biology, and chemistry of materials, nanoscience, and many other disciplines. The AFM is a relatively simple microscope, which uses touch detection to generate three-dimensional images of surfaces with a very high resolution. It is common for AFM to be use to visualize atoms, molecules, proteins, and living cells.

The AFM consists of a rigid element with a small tip on the end that is mount on a piezoelectric crystal in the form of a tube. The crystal will expand and contract proportionally according to the applied voltage. When voltage is apply to one of the electrodes, the crystal will contract or expand and this movement is register with a laser. The laser beam bounces off the rigid element and deviates up and down, according to the surface height map. This process can be describe using the analogy of a gramophone, whereby the player needle moves over the protuberances in the grooves of a vinyl record. As the tip of the AFM scans the sample surface, its displacements are recorded, from which a three-dimensional surface map is been constructed.

The tip of the AFM is extremely sensitive to the small forces acting on it (as small as 1 pico-Newton or 0.000000000001 N), and can be considered as a small "nano-scale finger" that can literally "feel" the structure of the surface, and capture the movement that takes place on the surface of an object (29). Consequently, it can determine the vibrational state of the object and the frequency it is emitting.

As research progresses with the use of new devices, it will be possible to measure the different frequencies emanating from the human body, down to the cellular level. There is the knowledge today for understanding the normal or stable ranges of each part of the body. With this information, different methods of exposure to external frequencies can be apply, allowing the affected component to restore its equilibrium state.

For thousands of years, sound has been consider a healing energy. It has been use in many ancient cultures and traditions for this purpose. Ancient civilizations that still exist today recognize its remarkable healing powers.

There are many old stories that show the healing power of sound. We can read in the Bible how the depression of King Saul was cure by David's harp. There is also an Egyptian papyrus dating back some 2600 years back that refers to the songs as an extraordinary treatment for sterility and rheumatic pain.

The early Greeks believed that music had a strong energy that can heal both the body and the soul. Gout and back pain were treated by the music produced by the lyre and the flute. It is known that the madness of Alexander the Great was cure by the melody played on the lyre. That has led to an ancient Greek adage that says, "Men have a song as a doctor for pain." Pythagoras, a well-known Greek philosopher, is also consider the father of music therapy. He believed in the power of sounds and made use of different songs and spells with specific melodies and rhythms, as they were effective in curing diseases of the body and mind.

In the temple of Dendera in Egypt (30), there is the following inscriptions:
- "The sky and the stars play music for you"
- "The Sun and the Moon praise you"
- "The gods sing for you"

The temple of Dendera was dedicate to Athor, the goddess of music and transformation, in addition to love and fertility. In this temple, they found the zodiac of Dendera, together with different musical instruments that were venerated. Athor, similar to the Hindu goddess Vac, is the mother of the voice and thus sound.

The Corpus Hermeticum also contains a reference to the use of sound by the Egyptians as something other than words. The book, written in the first century AD, was part of an original one, possibly dating back to 1400 BC.

The Egyptians believed that vowel sounds were sacred, due to which their written hieroglyphic language contains no vowels. Therefore, we can safely assume that the singing of the vowels had a powerful meaning for their priests.

The Egyptian priestesses used the sistrum, a musical instrument with metal discs that creates not only a pleasant sound but also, as we now know, generates large amounts of ultrasound.

Ultrasound is an effective healing modality, which currently is been used in hospitals and clinics. Hence, it is very possible that the sistrum was use in ceremonies not only to improve the sound, but also with the intention of healing.

In a letter to King Amman, Asclepius said, "As for us, we do not use simple words, but the power of all sounds" (the power of the word).

If we refer to the Bible, in John 1: 1, we can find the following references:

- In the beginning was the Word,
- and the Word was with God,

- and the Word was God.

Just to mention someone that follow this tradition today, Ani Williams is a musician and composer who interprets music that not only comforts the hearing, but also contains some therapeutic component (32).

We know that the voice generates a sound, which is essentially a vibration. Depending on what is been said and how it is been said, different ranges of vibration are produced, which have certain effect. Human voice, music, and all other sounds are part of the whole; everything is related, connected and interacting with all living beings.

Healing with sound is the beneficial application of sound frequencies to heal the mind and body. It aims bring the person to a state of harmony and good health. It is both strange and interesting to note that, in ancient times, techniques based on sound were used to restore balance in the body, apparently without having the technical information that is available today.

Having too much interference from our environment affect us, and lowering to a minimum this exchange, in some cases could be beneficial. There is a technique called "sensory isolation." The base of this technique works by creating an environment blocking any condition that stimulate the senses. This practice works based on sensory isolation tanks containing salt water at a temperature equal to that of the human body. The water has the same specific density that the composition of the human body, which causes the body to float naturally. The tanks are located in a completely dark room, isolated from any noise. They are been use for short periods as a relaxation method.

According to the findings yielded by extant experiments, staying in this environment for long periods produces hallucinations and psychological disorders. This same effect is achieve when prisoners are place in solitary confinement, as the conditions is such cells are similar to sensory deprivation, without the comfort of floating on water. Still, their effects confirm that prolonged isolation is a punishment for both the body and the mind.

Silence in a natural environment is compensate by vision and touch, whereas vision could be replace by sound and touch. The total lack of sensory stimulation creates an imbalance in the mental functioning of the human being. It is clear that we cannot live in isolation and that we have to be "connected" and "interact" with everything that surrounds us.

In relating to this point with astrology, can be mention that the planetary influence of the natal chart, the different planetary transits, and aspects, all come from outside ourselves, and should be consider part of our "environment."

The existence of things is based on a certain vibration, and astrology is not outside of this universal mechanics. The interpretation of the natal chart, transits, and other astral influences will obviously depend on the knowledge, analysis and perception of the astrologer. However, if in addition to this the astrologer also could have "technical" information resulting from the measurement of the "person's environment," this could be the next evolutionary step in astrology.

Just to reaffirm that is possible to measure anything, let us consider the following report that the government of the United States made public.

In 2003, the CIA (Central Intelligence Agency of the United States) declassified a secret study conducted in the 1980s. In this study related to subject no so common such as astral travel, telepathy, and the power of thoughts, among others. The objective of the study was gather information that could be used for intelligence and military purposes. The information contained in this report explains many of the things called "esoteric," with analysis and fundamentals that show that not all things are, as they are commonly understood. For example, the findings indicate that is possible to measure thoughts. That they can be projected, and directed toward a certain objective.

Just to mention something that is happening today's day, a company in China is "collecting thoughts" from employees and storing them in a database. We need to speculate that they are collecting brain waves and translating them into something meaningful to the point that they can be stored.

In the 1960s, intensive studies and tests were carried out, mainly in the United States and the USSR, on what is call "remote vision." The method consist on mentalizing a person, who was able to mentally "move" to another place for observing and making a description of the remote surroundings. Successful experiences were achieve in this aspect, prompting further extension of the study, whereby one person would remotely "insert" thoughts or ideas to another person's mind. As strange as this sounds, this happened and it was documented (33).

Understanding the basis of the functioning of things, as well as the implications that each thought, intention, or action has on each person, is essential to be able to return to the source of the natural order and functioning of both our environment and ourselves.

The objective here is not to enter into complex issues, that the reader may or may not be aware of, but merely to prompt us to open our minds and understand that we are surrounded by things usually not been considered. Thighs that we do not see, that we are not aware or do not realize, but are still happening and are part of our reality and environment.

The more we understand how the universe works and appreciate our role in it, the more possibilities we will have to find a solution to each problem and with them move forward in our evolution.

Summary of this section

Sounds that can heal. This statement may sound very simple, or you may take it as a quackery. Still, the question we have to ask is, why is that through the ages—from the Bible, going through the Egyptians, Greeks, Romans, Tibetan monks, Australian natives, in Sufi and Kabbalistic practices to this day—people have been aware of the healing property of certain sounds? Is it that ancient civilizations, as well as the scholars and enlightened individuals from different eras, had nothing better to do than practice or talk about these nonsense theories? No only we have to give them credit for their findings but also take our responsibility to research, understand and use if we feel convince enough.

For the inquisitive, awake, or evolutionary mind, nothing is superfluous; everything is a source of new information and knowledge. Thus, nothing should be dismiss without careful analysis and examination of findings. As mentioned on several occasions, we are different in some aspects, but also we share many similarities. For example, if standing under the rain, we will all get wet in the same way. With this simple example, we can see that, although we are different, there are things that affect us equally. We are constantly recipients of external inputs, of every part that makes up our environment, which influences us in some way.

We know that a certain natal aspect or planetary transit can affect our psyche or our body, and with the information shared so far, we can say that, if any part of our body does not work well, the energy/frequency mismatch is the cause.

It is important to clarify that a "natal" aspect could pertain to a deficiency in the original mechanism of the body, which cannot be address with the subject in discussion, since it would be consider a natural deficiency.

We can take an example the extreme case of been born with one leg shorter than the other. Without going into the detail of why this happened, there is not much that can be done about it, unless the individual is willing to undergo the immensely invasive procedure of bone breaking and ossification or get a shoe with a supplement to compensate the deficiency. This is to be consider a "basic structural" problem, not a functioning one. Thus, in this section, we focused on treatments for issues stemming from external influences, rather than congenital defects.

There are planetary transits that can alter our nerves, metabolism, appetite, and concentration, as well as cause a wide range of other issues that we have to face on a daily basis. The sonic healing that was mention aims to help us overcome those periods where some specific energies are active.

A transit that generates a nervous state, depending on the person and its ability to respond to stress, can end up in an accident, a burn, a broken bone, a tachycardia and many other conditions. Clearly, the issue would no longer be a nervous state, but the consequences that this can bring if not handled properly. This sums up the idea that together with the astrological evaluation, alternative methods to help overcome these periods are possible.

With this section, we finalize the evaluation of the frequencies and alternative methods to support temporary deviations, to pass to the next topic that, although it is new, is interesting to analyze and see how astrology fits into the new paradigm that is already part of our reality, organ transplant.

Organ Transplants and More

Astrology takes the natural development of pregnancy as the starting point, setting the position of the stars in the natal chart at birth.

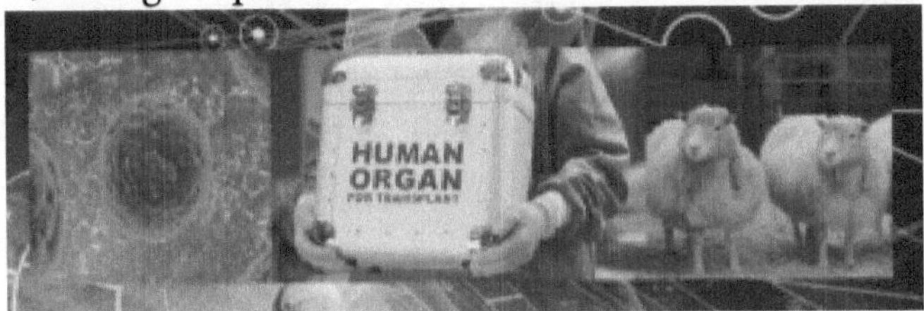

However, beyond being identified by our natal chart, each of us also carries with us the "experiences" of the nine months of pregnancy, along with the environment into which we are born and the genetic inheritance. All this makes up 100% of our being, which astrology interprets through the analysis of cycles.

Both our genetics and the period of pregnancy have a considerable weight in the essence of our core being, and may or may not be conditioning factors in our evolutionary process. The renowned psychiatrist Dr. Stanislav Grof in his book *When the Impossible Happens* makes a very detailed account of patients under his treatment in relation to the pregnancy period. Patient refer to daily situations, and certain experiences, for which they were not able to explain why they occur. After different analysis and practices, they found that patients perceived things related to the pregnancy period that they were not aware. For example, one patient under certain stressful situation was smelling leather, when nothing around would produce that. They found out that the pregnancy period was very stressful for the mother, and that she worked in a shop were leather was processed. The patient did not have any previous knowledge of that. This is an important aspect to understand, as our psychological development and our "formation" does not begin at birth, but at the moment of conception. In the context of astrology, in the natal chart, when certain sign, planets, and aspects, are present in House XII provides a clue of this type of situation.

The genetic part also is also important, since aspects or physical conditions of both the mother and the father could be inherited in different combinations or percentages. However, these percentages are still under science determination.

In the foregoing discussions, we will focus on the pregnancies involving surrogate mothers, the children of same-sex couples (as the mother and father as traditional astrology analyzes) and clones. In such cases, we are facing a very complex issue that departs from the traditional lines. As these are also relatively new phenomena, there is no specialized information on the subject. Still, given their growing number of this situation and meaning at the social level, it would be interesting to see where astrology positioned itself with respect to these themes.

Another aspect to consider is that of transplants. Would a heart transplant affect the cycles of the birth chart? In what way are the donor cycles influence the recipient? Should the astrologer have the donor's information, beyond the fact that person is no alive, in order to consider all the factors in the analysis? The same would apply for a transplant of liver, kidney or any other organ.

As progress is made in medical field, organ transplants are been performed as a normal practice and can no longer be considered an exception. Dr. Christian Barnard performed the first heart transplant in Cape Town in 1967. Since then, immense advances have been made in the transplant and rehabilitation techniques that extend to other organs of the body. In addition, research into stem cells and organ regeneration in animals continues, aiming to produce a ready supply of organs that can be transplant into humans.

Organ donation is nonetheless still a controversial subject and, while in most countries, an individual has to specifically declare willing to be an organ donor upon death, in some countries, everyone is considered an organ donor unless they 'opt out' of the system. As population ages and the need for organs increases, it is possible that the latter approach will become the standard in the not too distant future.

These topics are included in the present discussion because, in astrology, the transplanted organ is govern by the donor's natal chart. This prompts the question of how an aspect of a planetary transit of the native with respect to the implanted organ can be analyze.

Each organ is in the process of continuous regeneration, and depending on the organ or tissue; it could take months or years to be completely replace (34).

In the book *Change of Heart*, published in London in 1998, the authors Claire Sylvia and William Novak recount the experiences of patients who had heart transplants. After a transplant, the physical body of the recipient resumes its normal functioning, but the psychological aspect is influence by the personal characteristics of the donor. It seems that, over time, this behavior is level and the persons who received the transplant take full control of their psychological aspect, but some of the donor's characteristics can get incorporated into their personality (35).

Some of the experiences reported in the book mentioned below.

A transplant nurse from Florida told us that a heart transplant patient, who, before her operation, suffered from extreme fear of water, soon after the transplant, this same person, felt a great desire to go swimming and sailing. A surgical resident doctor, who knew the background of the donor, informed the woman's unbelieving family that her donor had been an avid sailor who died in a boating accident.

The same nurse told us about a fifty-something-year-old man who received a new heart from a young donor who was killed in a motorcycle accident. The receiver, a Christian who was reborn, woke up from the operation cursing and insulting, which was completely out of character. Because the donor had died in the same hospital where the transplant was done, the donor's mother ended up finding the recipient. She confirmed that the man was speaking like his son, and was even using some of his terms.

A number of physicians came to our institute and over the years and, I have heard other stories like this. A heart surgeon told me that he has observed this phenomenon, which includes changes in personality and desire for new foods and that this often fades a few months after the transplant, it's not something surgeons want publicity for, and they keep it very quiet.

Mental and physical influence of the organ donor on the recipient

The mental influence in the recipient is been stated, by the knowledge of new subjects that did not know before, in addition to the physical influences such as the way of walking of the dead donor. The personality of a female recipient was change, having a masculine turn, she felt more secure, firm and energetic, and felt that she knew issues that only men knew, a knowledge that strangely came to her from some unknown source.

Even in her way of walking was manly. "Mom," the daughter said, "Why are you walking like that? You are staggering like if you are a football player.

The new masculine energy was not limited to her step of walking. In addition as stated by her, the new way of walking was a metaphor for the way she now moved around the world, without feeling limited. She felt a new power that was associated with vibration, strength and masculinity.

While there is enough information related to how the recipient of a donation can react, this not an issue discussed openly. From the point of view of astrology, it is important to consider how this situation would be analyze, as from the moment a person receives a new organ, in this specific case the heart, this can have significant relevance in future cycles of the person, when transits and aspects related are activated.

Other organs are also important, such as the liver and kidneys, for example, but the heart is fundamental in many aspects beyond being the vital organ in the human body.

Since 1988, In the United States alone, 683,000 transplants were perform, with an exponential increase in recent years (36).

Summary of this section

Astrology presents a position in relation to the human body, where each part of the body is associated with an astrological sign. It is widely established that each sign is associated with one or more planets of the Solar System. By analyzing the natal chart, the houses and zodiacal signs the astrologer can determine the ones with additional "load" in relation to their aspects.

Let us take the heart as an example; it is govern by the sign of Leo and by the Sun. For a person to have reached the point of needing a heart transplant, the natal chart should have strong indications that this was possible. At this point, it is worth mentioning that we are talking about an adult person and not the replacement of the heart of an infant who was already born with a congenital heart defect.

Given the existence in the natal chart indicating a potential heart problem, if the person did not take any action to counteract that "bad aspect," this could determine the extreme situation that came consequently. However, what about the future of the person living with that "new" heart? Will such an individual continue to be govern by the original natal conditions? The first response to that will be yes, but what role the new heart will play?

A person who undergoes a transplant surgery will have a very strict recovery process, and will go through a monitoring process for some time, both on the clinical aspect than for the way of life. If the person was previously prone to excesses, these will have to change. Regular physical activity, nutritious diet, and alcohol and tobacco abstinence are among the subjects that will be under strict supervision as a part of the recovery treatment.

Continuing with the analysis, the heart that was "influenced" by the original natal aspects died and it was replaced. The heart that was transplanted is still alive, although the body from which it came no longer exists. By the astrological guidelines, this heart is govern by the natal chart of the person who donated the organ and not by the one who receives it.

A planetary transits can be done for a natal chart for before birth as well as after death, and in fact this was mentioned in the discussion of the cycles, to demonstrate that cycles were already functioning before we were born, and will continue to operate even when we have departed from this physical plane.

According to these premises, and taking only the mechanical functioning of the human body into consideration, the transplanted heart would have to continue to function under the aspects of its original birth chart. As a result, when planetary transits of the recipient of the transplant are analyze, transits of the transplanted organ should also be taken into account for a complete evaluation of the intervening cycles. Taking into consideration that part of the psychological aspects are passed on from the donor to the recipient, which tend to disappear or minimize over time, it would be necessary to determine for how long both cycles are active.

Life is been simplified in many aspects, but as you can see, scientific advances exert an impact on our way of life. Hence, astrology requires an adaptation to the current situation in order to preserve what it represents.

This was only the beginning because, as we will see in the next section, with artificial intelligence (AI), things take an unimaginable dimension.

AI, Intelligent Prostheses, and Robots

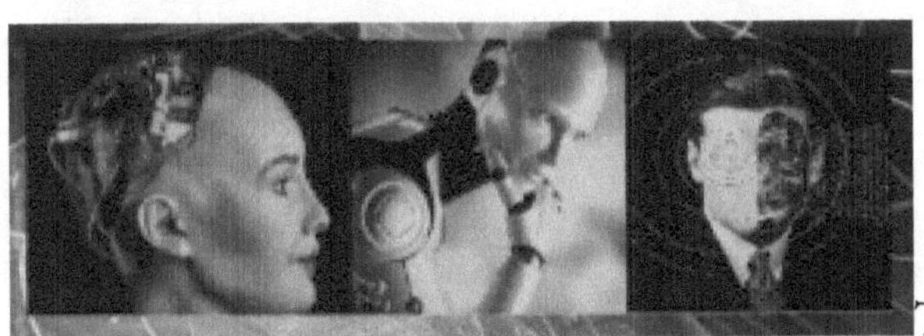The term "Artificial Intelligence" was coined by John McCarthy in 1956 as the science and engineering of making intelligent machines. Since then, the technological advances have reached a point where something that, not long ago was consider science fiction, has become reality. In 1996, IBM Deep Blue computer won a chess match against Russian chess grandmaster Garry Kasparov. Since that event, the advancement of intelligent systems has been astronomical.

Modern AI systems have the peculiarity of receiving information from their environment through different types of sensors, in the same way that a person receives them through its senses. At the same time, they have access to any information available on the Internet, regardless of the language. These systems have integrated language translators (similar to the Google translator, for example) with which they can search and analyze the information regardless of the language of origin.

Those who use Google's email would have noticed that, when they receive an email, at the time of answering, the system would offer different options for responding. Moreover, when you start writing the answer, the system will anticipate the rest of the sentence and by pressing the space bar the sentence will be automatically fill.

The email from arrival goes to a process starting by interpreting the content (beyond the language) for building and proposing a response. I doubt that anyone has stopped to ponder on the magnitude of the speed, hardware, and programming required not only to interpret the content of the email, but also to provide an answer. When this process is concurrently been used by billions of users around the world, it is difficult for the mind to comprehend the level of complexity magnitude of the task.

It is worth noting that all the information involved in these interactions is save and use for analysis and development of future automatic responses. That means that the systems have stored all the emails regardless their status. Everything is information and everything serves to evaluate future actions.

Email is just one aspect of many that rely on a similar process. For example, Google keeps track of phones, regardless of the phone as long as their applications are in use, and stores the information of all the movements of the device and therefore the person using it (geolocation). It stores the information in real time regarding the location when the device moves, tracking the path that it takes, the speed at which it is moving and by correlation with geolocation maps, public places, shops, or private places visited. It is worth remembering that all this information is been stored.

Facebook and other social networks work in a similar way, with the addition that they have the connection between personal relationships, along with their personal preferences.

At this point, you may be wondering what this has to do with astrology. Would it be very repetitive to say that EVERYTHING is part of the WHOLE and EVERYTHING is related?

In the 1980s, personal computers become popular, prompting the development of the systems related to astrology. For those who are not familiar with the process of making a natal chart, it is worth mentioning that tables called ephemerides are used, which contain the information on the daily positions of the planets in the Solar System. The ephemerides can start from some year B.C. and extend far into the future, such as the year 2050. This can give an idea of the size of these tables and the amount of information they contain. In addition, to make the birth chart, we must consider the summer light saving time for countries that implement this modality or did so in some period in the past. If this is not consider in the calculation, the definitions of the ascendant and the houses will be wrong. Moreover, the list of all the towns and cities of all countries on Earth with the longitude, latitude, and time difference relative to the Greenwich meridian must be included.

The rising sign is calculated with this information, along with the mid heaven, the distribution of the houses and positions of the planets in them, as well as the aspects that the planets have among themselves.

All this was already possible by personal systems 35 years ago, even if they were very limited in their capacity. Nowadays you can go to any of the multiple Internet sites that offer these services or you can buy such systems for personal use.

What is the next step for astrology with respect to artificial intelligence?

AI can integrate an astrology system and obtain the following:

1. Everything that exists on the Internet related to astrology regardless of the language (books, blogs, web pages, social networks, etc.).
2. All personal information available in terms of tastes, activities, family, friends, profession, work, restaurants, movies, sports, vacation spots, illnesses, and everything related to the person's past and present.
3. Social, political, and economic conditions of the place of residence for the existing news on the Internet (past and present).

There are already AI systems in use in Japan, where the employer decides whether to consider a candidate for a job according to the future evolution that the system predicts for that person. The system makes the search in all available information and gives a projection over the possible scenarios over time; in other words, based on what the person has done previously, it predicts the future. This and other applications already in use today demonstrate the level of penetration of such practices (37).

According to a recent article from the UK, artificial intelligence will start to be use in the prevention of crimes (38). In the movie "Minority Report" released in 2002, the subject was presented as science fiction, but as we can see, it became reality only 16 years later.

After what it was mention, is there any doubt that the future of astrology is based on artificial intelligence?

Artificial intelligence will not only be able to generate the natal chart and perform other common astrological evaluations, but, with all the information available about the person, the system will be able to relate the past periods and perform an evaluation and predict the most possible outcome for the future. Based on this, you can forecast with a certain degree of accuracy the future actions of the individual under the future astrological cycles.

The crime prevention application is taking into consideration future possible actions of an individual, based on past actions and the current situation or environment. Is there any difference in the procedure?

Not only is it possible to determine future actions given the evaluation of past information, but, with the processing performed by artificial intelligence, future actions could be recommended for avoiding problems, including interactions within existing personal relationships, since the cycles of the other persons can be included within the analysis.

In this analysis, one could compare the natal charts of different persons (Synastry), focusing on their own transits and of the ones of the persons that form the related circle in the social, work and family networks. You have to remember that all the personal information, although it is not accessible to any person; it can be access by an AI systems.

In order to be able to comprehend the power of AI, it is worth noting that, at the artificial intelligence laboratory of Facebook, they performed a test where two systems (with access to all the information on the Internet) were communicating through questions and answers. At a certain point in the conversation, and to the astonishment of those who monitored the test, the systems began to communicate in a language that only both systems could interpret (39). The technicians canceled the test as a prevention, given that they lost control of the evaluation because they could not interpret the conversation held by the two intelligent systems.

Intelligent Prostheses

Science and technology have advanced considerably, particularly in the miniaturization of microchips, which has made it possible to replace missing parts of the body (mainly arms and legs) with intelligent mechanical parts, which integrate into the nervous system of the body.

There is a type of prosthesis are powered by high-power batteries and their mechanisms respond based on the electrical impulses of the nervous system, producing movements similar to those of the natural limb. When an implant of this type is applied, the recipient must go through a period of training and adaptation to be able to control it (40).

From the astrological perspective, there are two ways for its analysis, focusing on the reason for the loss of the limb, and considering the prosthesis as an integrated replacement of a natural limb. It is worth to mention again, that a zodiacal sign rules each part of the human body.

The natal chart can provide some reference of the conditions that might lead to the loss of a limb. For a case as extreme as the one mentioned, a very powerful planetary transit would be required, and the natal chart would indicate some conditions that could cause this to happen. It can be a subject of debate if the person could have prevented that loss through a previous personal work for compensating the bad natal aspect.

As defined by Dr. Adler, if we consider the evolutionary meaning for each planet in the personal natal chart the "negative" consequence of a given natal aspect or transit, could be represented in extreme situations, such as loss of a limb. If this were the case, the loss of the limb and replacement by another only helps to maintain the operative aspect of the body, but it would be necessary to see how the person evolves after the replacement in the remaining aspects. This is similar to what was mention on the heart transplant.

If we accept this as a definition, the implanted prosthesis would have to follow the same "astrological rules" as the limb it replaced, beyond the prosthesis having a date of its own creation, which gives it certain "personal" aspects, whereby we would have to see how it integrates in the evaluation of future transits.

Robots

Here a similar situation to the one related to intelligent prostheses arises, as there is no information or antecedent of how astrology determines the probable possibilities within the cycles. Taking into consideration that is possible to construct the natal chart with the date and time of the robot's creation or departure from the factory. Each element has a time stamp.

Astrology allows the creation of a birth chart for various things and elements beyond people, but the case we are dealing with—this "element," the robot—is composed of something more than physical parts, since it contains a software with the possibility of evolving by acquiring new knowledge. It will initially act based on the basic knowledge programmed, but it will undergo a continuous learning process, capitalizing on everything previously learned. This growth has no limit except for the physical capacity that was assign originally to the device or system.

We are in front of an element that was created at a certain moment, which has the possibility of increasing its "intelligence." As demonstrated by the study carried out by Facebook (similar experiences happen for Google and Microsoft), at a certain moment AI systems have the freedom to create something completely new, by using the acquired knowledge.

Similar to what was envisioned in science fiction films like "Terminator" and others, and at the time seemed like a good imaginative plot, but now we are seeing it materialize before our eyes.

In the same way that a person at birth brings a base given by the genetic inheritance and experience of the months of pregnancy, a system of this type goes through a similar process of manufacturing of its physical aspects and programming from the point of view of learning, analysis, and operation.

With respect to the issue of manufacturing, robots can go through manufacturing processes like any other element (something physical), and are composed of different parts that will have their periods of stress depending on the transits that are active based on the natal chart based on the manufacturing date.

Unlike the programming part (logical operation), although it has its "birth" with the same day of manufacture, this has its own development. In this case, the programming should not be consider under the same analysis as the mechanical parts since, as mentioned above, the system starts from a basic programming, but continues to evolve through learning. From the moment that this process begins, the system started its evolutionary learning process.

Put it in another way, the robot will have a natal chart that includes its physical part and its logical part, but the logical part would be impacted by the evolutionary processes that comply with all the steps of the evolutionary processes of the person (from the mental point of view).

This approach may be preposterous for anyone who does not have knowledge on the subject, but we have to take into consideration that this is a reality already present in our society and integrated into our daily lives. Only 30 years ago, the cell phone was only a matter of science fiction movies and today it is part of our daily life. The phones already have a limited artificial intelligence, even if we are not aware of these capabilities.

A robot is a device that has functions of movement and action handled by an artificial intelligence, while artificial intelligence is a system that can work without having to produce a movement or product, as its primary aim is to process information and represent it in devices such as monitors, telephones, cars, airplanes, appliances, and others.

Summary of this section

Someone may think that this section should have been the first one, since it presents a panorama quite different from what anyone would expect. However, the analysis began with the functioning of the human body because this is the base, it is the center, and it is the reason for astrology and everything that may come. If we stop considering the human being, astrology no longer has a purpose.

Something that has to be clear is that information is just that, information. The information used with consciousness and intelligence and then represented by action, becomes wisdom. Regardless of whether the information comes from a book, a person, or artificial intelligence, we are the ones who ultimately have the capacity and the power to use it.

Everything begins and ends with us; the stars can provide guidance, but we determine which path we take, based on the options presented. No machine or system can replace us in our way of thinking, feeling, and acting. However, let us be clear, this is not given freely; first, we have to be aware and accept our responsibility. For a number of reasons, it can be more comfortable replacing our thinking with that of an artificial intelligence, and letting it tell us what to say, what to answer and what to do. However, we have to understand that, if we give our "thinking" to an AI system, what will happen to our feelings? What will happen to our actions?

We found ourselves on a critical path. We are face with this dilemma, because at this instance, if we give our actions to AI, we would cease to exist as superior and individual entities and we would simply become robots.

Assigning Values in Astrology

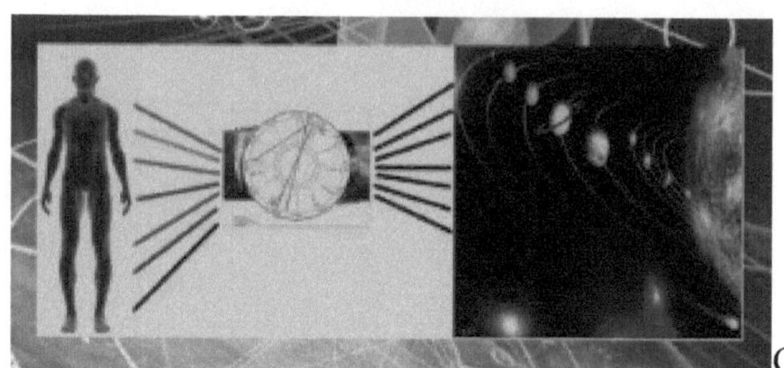

Over the centuries, astrologers have searched for a reliable method to evaluate or measure planetary energies or strengths by assigning scores or values based on certain dignifying or debilitating factors; after all, the numbers are everywhere in the Universe. According to the 11th-century Arab astrologer, Al-Biruni, this was a common practice among the Babylonians and Persians, who compared the total scores assigned to individual planets to discover which was the most prominent. This was then known as the Almuten (from Arabic: al-mateen, meaning 'the firm' or 'strong in power'), or Lord of Geniture (or Nativity), and particular consideration was given to its powerful influence in the definition of the temperament and observable features of an individual.

Ptolemy created a table of values depending on certain aspects and characteristics, and later William Lilly (renowned English astrologer who lived between 1602 and 1681) created a new evaluation system (41).

The modern simplification of the natal technique, which assigns the "Ruler of the Chart" title to the planet that governs the sign in the ascendant, will obviously not succeed as the correct approach, if the magnifying and weakening factors are not been taking into consideration. planet It is essential in the hourly charts the consideration of the sensitivity of the planet to the general condition.

On page 115 of the *Christian Astrology*, Lilly created a table of factors to consider when determining the strengths and weaknesses of the planets. According to this approach, the numerical scores vary from +38 for an extremely dignified planet to -38 for a severely weakened one. There are similar tables with various adaptations, whereby some assign dignity to the planets in their ruling house, and detract from the planets in houses opposite their ruling house. Some give values for planets that increase in northern latitude and subtract it for planets that increase in southern latitude. In general, it is important to understand that these tables exist as a guide for the analysis, not as a substitute for the general interpretation.

The important thing to note here is that, from ancient times, the astrologers tried to find a "methodology" for mathematically evaluating the natal chart and the planets. Although interpretation is a very important factor in the analysis of a natal chart or a transit, assigning value to these elements could make the interpretation more accurate.

Table created by William Lilly with the values of the planets depending on the sign and its position.

TABLE OF THE ESSENTIAL DIGNITIES OF THE PLANETS, &c.

Signs	Houses	Exaltations	Triplicity Day	Triplicity Night	Terms					Faces			Detriment	Fall
♈	♂ D.	☉ 19	☉	♃	♃ 6	♀ 14	☿ 21	♂ 26	♄ 30	♂ 10	☉ 20	♀ 30	♀	♄
♉	♀ N.	☽ 3	♀	☽	♀ 8	☿ 15	♃ 22	♄ 20	♂ 30	☿ 10	☽ 20	♄ 30	♂	
♊	☿ D.	☊ 3	♄	☿	☿ 7	♃ 14	♀ 21	♄ 25	♂ 30	♃ 10	♂ 20	☉ 30	♃	
♋	☽ D./N.	♃ 15	♂	♂	♂ 6	♃ 13	☿ 20	♀ 27	♄ 30	♀ 10	☿ 20	☽ 30	♄	♂
♌	☉ D./N.		☉	♃	♄ 6	☿ 13	♀ 19	♃ 25	♂ 30	♄ 10	♃ 20	♂ 30	♄	
♍	☿ N.	☿ 15	♀	☽	☿ 7	♀ 13	♃ 18	♄ 24	♂ 30	☉ 10	♀ 20	☿ 30	♃	♀
♎	♀ D.	♄ 21	♄	☿	♄ 6	♀ 11	♃ 19	☿ 24	♂ 30	☽ 10	♄ 20	♃ 30	♂	☉
♏	♂ N.		♂	♂	♂ 6	♃ 14	♀ 21	☿ 27	♄ 30	♂ 10	☉ 20	♀ 30	♀	☽
♐	♃ D.	☋ 3	☉	♃	♃ 8	♀ 14	☿ 19	♄ 25	♂ 30	☿ 10	☽ 20	♄ 30	☿	
♑	♄ N.	♂ 28	♀	☽	♀ 6	☿ 12	♃ 19	♂ 25	♄ 30	♃ 10	♂ 20	☉ 30	☽	♃
♒	♄ D.		♄	☿	♄ 6	☿ 12	♀ 20	♃ 25	♂ 30	♀ 10	☿ 20	☽ 30	☉	
♓	♃ N.	♀ 27	♂	♂	♀ 8	♃ 14	☿ 20	♂ 26	♄ 30	♄ 10	♃ 20	♂ 30	☿	☿

Las Características Planetarias en cuanto a su domicilio en la carta con valores:

	DOMICILIO	EXILIO	EXALTADO	CAIDA
SOL	LEO +5	ACUARIO	ARIES +4	LIBRA -4
LUNA	CANCER +5	CAPRICORNIO	TAURO +4	ESCORPIO -4
MERCURIO	GEMINIS & VIRGO +5	SAGITARIO & PISCIS	ACUARIO +4	LEO
VENUS	TAURO & LIBRA +5	ESCORPIO & ARIES	PISCIS +4	VIRGO -4
MARTE	ARIES & ESCORPIO +5	LIBRA & TAURO	CAPRICORNIO +4	CANCER -4
JUPITER	SAGITARIO & PISCIS +5	GEMINIS & VIRGO	CANCER +4	CAPRICORNIO -4
SATURNO	CAPRICORNIO & ACUARIO +5	CANCER & LEO	LIBRA +4	ARIES -4
URANO	ACUARIO +5	LEO	ESCORPIO +4	TAURO
NEPTUNO	PISCIS +5	VIRGO	CANCER +4	CAPRICORNIO
PLUTON	ESCORPIO +5	TAURO	PISCIS +4	VIRGO

According to the table, the planets that are in the sign of 'domicile' or 'exalted' will be given greater weight within the chart, whereas those that are in a sign of 'exile' or 'fall' will have lower energetic value or weight.

Table of points for Exaltation or Weaknesses by Sign, created by William Lilly

SIGNO	Domicilio +5	Exaltacion +4	Detrimento −5	Caida −4
♈	♂	☉	♀	♄
♉	♀	☽	♂	
♊	☿	☊	♃	☋
♋	☽	♃	♄	♂
♌	☉		♄	
♍	☿	☿	♃	♀
♎	♀	♄	♂	☉
♏	♂		♀	☽
♐	♃	☋	☿	☊
♑	♄	♂	☽	♃
♒	♄		☉	
♓	♃	♀	☿	☿

Among the planets, the most influential are those that are located:

- on or near the Ascendant (House I)

- in or near MC Midheaven, at the beginning of House X

- in or near or from the DC Descendant (House VI)

If there were no planets in any of the points of the natal chart mentioned above, the planet with more weight would be the ruler of the ascendant.

Triplicity (considering the sign and the time of day)

	SIGNO	Dariot Dia	Dariot NOCHE	Dariot INTERC.	Lilly Dia	Lilly NOCHE
Fuego	♈ ♌ ♐	☉	♃	♄	☉	♃
Tierra	♉ ♍ ♑	♀	☽	♂	♀	☽
Aire	♊ ♎ ♒	♄	☿	♃	♄	☿
Agua	♋ ♏ ♓	♀	♂	☽	♂	♂

Table of Decanates used by William Lilly

	Día	Noche
Fuego	Sol	Júpiter
Tierra	Venus	Luna
Aire	Saturno	Mercurio
Agua	Marte	Marte

When in correspondence +1 is add to the calculation

Tabla de William Lilly para evaluar la Fortaleza o Debilidad de cada Planeta

Fortaleza Básica (+)

En su signo o en recepción mutual con otro planeta por el signo	5
En fortaleza, o recepción mutual de fortaleza	4
En su propia triplicidad	3
En sus propios términos	2
Anti si	1

Debilidad Básica (-)

en Detrimento	-5
en Caída	-4
Peregrino	-5

Fortalezas Accidentales (+)

En las casas 10 o 1	5
En las casas 7, 4, o 11	4
En las casas 2 o 5	3
En las casa 9	2
En la casa 3	1
Directo en movimiento	4
Rápido en movimiento	2
Saturno, Júpiter, Marte cuando oriental	2
Mercury, Venus cuando Occidental	2
Luna en aumento de luz (creciente)	2
Libre de combustión y fuera del alcance del Sol	5
Cazimi (dentro de 0°17' del Sol)	5
Conjunción con Júpiter o Venus	5
Conjunción con el Nodo Norte	4
Trígono con Júpiter o Venus	4
Sextil con Júpiter o Venus	3
Conjunción con la estrella fija Regulus (29°40 Leo)	6
Conjunción con la Estrella fija Spica (23°40 Libra)	5

Debilidades Accidental (-)

En la casa 12	-5
En las casas 8 o 6	-2
Retrogrado	-5
Lento en movimiento	-2
Saturno, Júpiter, Marte cuando occidental	-2
Mercurio, Venus cuando oriental	-2
Luna en disminución de luz (menguante)	-2
Combustión (dentro de 8°30' del sol)	-5
Bajo los rayos del Sol (dentro de 17° del Sol)	-4
Conjunción con Saturno o Marte	-5
Conjunción con el Nodo Sur	-4
Conjunción con Saturno o Marte	-4
Oposición con Saturno o Marte	-4
Cuadratura con Saturno o Marte	-4
Conjunción con Algol o dentro de 5° (26°04 Taurus)	-4

Lilly developed a system that, while complex to understand, gives the parameters to measure the planets and positions in the natal chart. The weight assigned to the planets in the birth chart will determine their weight when evaluating the transits.

Without a doubt, if Lilly had had a computer, he could have done many tests and would have perfected the system according to the experience obtained with his consultants, since manually it is a complex and very long calculation process.

Just as an example, most modern computerized systems evaluate a natal chart using the values of the parameters created by William Lilly.

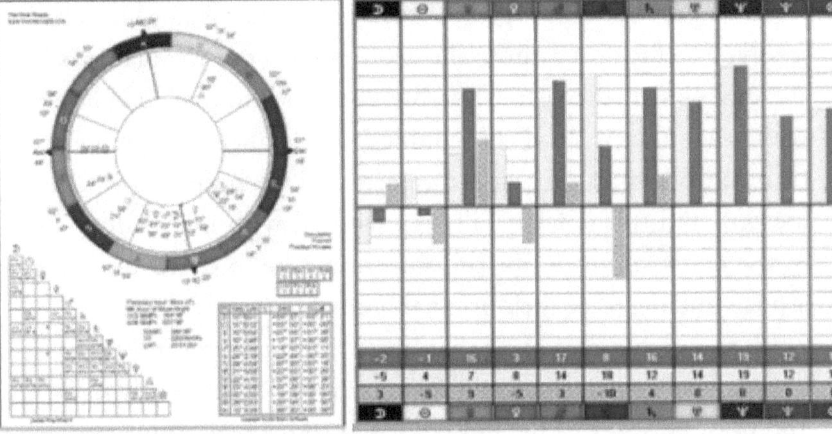

In short, astrologers who were famous for their knowledge and very successful in their practice looked for ways to evaluate astrology from a systematic point of view based on values, derived from experience, observations, and mathematical knowledge. Although from the technological point of view they were not up a level to understand how things work at the atomic level, today, as we saw in the points discussed above, there is information that could be applied to the evaluation and parameterization of the natal chart, aspects and cycles.

In the natal chart, beyond the astrological sign and the ascendant, there are signals that give a general view of the complications that the person must overcome during life. The birth chart contains basic information, which allows the astrologer to know the limitations and strengths of an individual. The aim of the valuation is to numerically represent these aspects.

Beyond the good or bad aspects or values that we can assign to the planets, we can mention Saturn and Neptune as good examples that can be numerically valued, since they determine the key aspects and characteristics of an individual. Each planet is important in the natal chart and none can be exclude from the analysis, but Saturn and Neptune could have a burden or value that affects the wellbeing and psyche the most. Uranus and Pluto also have cycles that can produce tremendous transformation and may or may not have a "heavy" load from its origin.

As a person's life progresses, each planet may change its "elevated" or "evolved" value or may not. The evolved aspect of the planet is in which the energies of the planet are present in a "mature" or "develop" way, while the other is "load" or "conflict". The planets can present a burden from the beginning, given the aspects and the houses in which they are located, and this is what Lilly represented with their values. However, in the course of one's life, the aim should be to overcome the negative aspects and decrease their original burden.

It is worth mentioning that some "conditioning" may exist at birth, but each person has the potential for developing and evolving during life, and must be aware of the limitations. If someone is only 5 feet tall (1.52 meters) and aspires to be a basketball player, the outcome in this domain will probably not be very successful. If we had unrealistic expectations, the frustrations that the person will go through, will not only impact sport, but will also impact on other aspects of their life.

This can be observed in students changing their mayor halfway through a degree, once they realize that it is not what they want and they have to start again in another direction.

These are very simple examples, aimed to emphasize the importance of knowing yourself. If you know who you are, what you are, and what your weaknesses and strengths are, your decisions will be more in tune with your essence, and will facilitate your path of development.

Saturn, which has a preponderant weight, will have a score according to the house in which it is located, as well as the aspects that it has. In the natal chart, it represents low vibration, indicating that it is the heavy backpack to carry, it is the test to overcome, and it is the teacher. The house represents the theme that we will have to manage or overcome. Depending on the positive or negative aspects for planets that go from the Sun to Mars, it will be the additional load or decrease of it. This is a good example where the concept of valorization can be very useful.

It is not the same a standalone Saturn in a certain house, that a Saturn with a square with the Sun or the Moon, for example. The differences when certain transits are active are substantial. The implications will be greater during this period.

It is very important that the individual can have this information, since Saturn will present complicated aspects in 7-year intervals. The evolutionary aspect with respect to Saturn, it is particular to the understanding of its implications. The person has to develop the techniques to cope with the complicated periods, knowing in advance, in what period these aspects will be active. In the same way, the person will have to take advantage when the transits are favorable, for consolidating things.

The other planet worthy of specific consideration is Neptune, the god of the sea, ruler of storms, liquids, unclear things, as well as source of inspiration and creativity, and of superior connection. Neptune is included because although it was not consider in antiquity, it is common to see its strong negative aspect when active in its lower development level.

Neptune in its non-evolved aspect can be represented as an unsafe person, with excessive use of medications (self-medication), unconventional drug use, dishonest or with few scruples in actions, just to mention a few. A person that has some of these characteristics is very likely unsuccessful and is still in the evolutionary process. Any type of "dependence" speaks of a person stuck in a certain moment of life which was not been able to leave behind (detach).

It is like a smoker who says, "I smoke, but I can quit smoking whenever I want."

Not only does this show that the person is "conditioned" by tobacco, but that he/she is also self-deceived in his/her ability to act. Self-deception is most probably not limited to tobacco only, but is reflected in other behavior patterns that in turn affect other aspects of the person and his/her evolutionary process.

Like other planets, it is important to see the house where Neptune is located and its aspects with other planets. Unlike Saturn, Neptune's energies can become low vibrations, and they are not materialize instantly in the material world. It will act like water, not as a tsunami, but rather as a filtration, going little by little until it shows when the damage was done.

Due to its characteristics, the evolutionary process of a poorly aspected Neptune requires much more mental work than Saturn. Once the person is aware on the subject to work on, there are many character correction methods that can be use, some of which require professional support and supervision. Like with Saturn, aspects with faster planets can present greater complications for the individual or provide a greater dose of creativity and spirituality.

Jupiter, defined as the opposite of Saturn, generates positive energy, which must also be manage, mainly due to the excesses in the material aspects that it may have if the energies are mismanage.

As an example of a type of valorization, and taking into account that each slow planet affects a different area of our evolutionary process, the assignment of value will be based on a scale depending on the position and aspects on the natal house.. This would determine the houses and aspects that will be activate according to the transits, considering the age that the person would have in each of them. If we consider Neptune transiting House VII when the person is seven years old, it will be markedly different relative to the same transits affecting a 40-year-old person.

In the book *Falling Upward* (Falling Up) by Richard Rohr, although this is written from the religious point of view and the Enneagram, the author states that a person can rarely start the evolutionary development before he/she is 42 years old. We are talking only about the beginning of this process, and this in no way indicates that it will actually begin, but that the conditions are propitious for starting the process. It is not by chance that, in astrology, this age coincides with the opposition of Uranus.

At this point, there is full coincidence with astrology, because as mentioned by Richard Rohr, you must have gone through and lived certain life experiences in order to understand how things are. In no way does this guarantee that the person will begin the evolutionary process, as someone can be 80 years old and continue without evolving. Still, after the opposition of Uranus, the conditions to begin this process are met. Let us clarify that the person is usually not aware of this. This period manifests itself with a need for change that cannot be explained, and if one is not careful, one can take a wrong direction in life. This is a period so critical in the development of each person, that it should be a matter of teaching and discussion during adolescence.

Summary of this section

Everything can be measured and evaluated, but this could be define as the "technical" aspect of something. The important thing is to consider what we can do with the information obtained.

In the evaluation of a natal chart, both an astrologer and an intelligent system can determine the values of each planet, house, and aspect. The result could be the same or one could provide more information than the other could, but the most important point to note is that the diagnostic information needs to be correctly interpret.

A large number of people go to astrologers or consult the stars on the Internet, but often do not consider the purpose of the consultation, or what to do with the information they obtained. What is the use of going to the doctor and doing a series of tests with the most sophisticated devices if afterwards the patient does not take the prescribed medicine?

Astrology has the ability to analyze the energy status of a person through its natal chart, from which the cycles and aspects formed follow, but we always arrive to the same fundamental point. The person is the one who will respond in one way or another, and will decide what to do with the information received.

A subject that was not mention, known as the "Solar Returns.", is highly important; these are the natal charts made for the birthday and represent the energies that will move in the year that is beginning. Its duration is approximately one year, and the person is able to change the position of the planets in the houses by varying the place of the birthday. That means that, when a certain planet will fall on the birthday in a house that for some reason one is trying to avoid (health/work, home, etc.), by changing the location at which to celebrate the birthday, the planets will move to another house. This technique puts the person in control of its path. The energies will be present (they cannot be avoided), but one has the power to direct them to the house with less impact.

The key cycles that determine the evolution of the person cannot be avoid, but as when one manages the weather forecast, one can prepare, especially for complicated periods. By the mere fact of being conscious and taking action based on the information received, shows that the person is aligned and on track in its evolutionary process.

Summary

Every morning the sun rises, whether we pay attention to it or not. Similarly, we can say that there will be a full moon, a waning quarter, a crescent or a new moon, and this we can do for the past as well as for the future. It is known when an eclipse will occur or when the planet Mars will be at its furthest or closest point from the Earth. You could continue listing infinite number of things and fill 100 sheets with events that have happened or will happen in the sky, with the exact date and time of their occurrence. The so-called Ephemerides provide part of this information.

You can determine the planetary transits for a person before he/she was born or after he/she has departed from this plane. This would not be very useful, but it highlights the fact that, regardless of one existence, all the processes in the Universe will continue to evolve according to very well established and predetermined cycles.

In stating this, I do not want to devalue the human being or anything that resembles that. On the contrary, I want to highlight the immensity of things that human beings have at their disposal in this life. There is an operating mechanism that gives you the magic of a sunrise, whether in the sea or on a mountain, or on the lonely streets of a city. From the rain to a sky full of stars, the caress of a breeze or the warm sensation of the sun in winter, and all the things that surround us that we usually ignore and we take for granted, there is a purpose for all things. There is a design, which our limited intelligence fails to understand in all its magnitude; we only grasp the idea through flashes that are presented to us from time to time.

This book has not created anything; it is just a compilation of information already available to anyone looking for it in books, lectures, videos, blogs, and articles, as shown in the references. In the same way that a long time ago a friend introduced me to astrology, and from that moment on I began my research to understand how it worked and what it was all about, each of us has the capacity to investigate and come to understand how any small part of this immense system works. In my particular case, I focus on astrology, but there is an infinite range of topics that can be research to understand in detail the functioning of things.

The important point to take away is that the answer is out there. If we do not understand why or how things work, starting with ourselves, with our character, our heritage, our formation, our physical part, our psyche, all we need to do is explore. If we do not know ourselves, what would remain for the rest of all the things around us and we interact daily?

As stated by renowned Swiss psychiatrist and psychoanalyst Carl Jung, "the one who looks outside dreams, the one who looks inside awakes." Any change we seek must begin by understanding what we are, how we function, and what motivates us, and then we can create the road map of the evolutionary path to follow, which is individual and at times can even be solitary. We are sparks of life, essence of the universe or individual universes, depending on how you want to see it. Still, whatever definition we give it, we cannot deny the greatness and immensity of the human being as part of a greater thing.

Finally, we have come to a subject that is not only fundamental, but is the purpose of life, which is evolution. This evolution can sometimes be supported by external circumstances, and could become so significant that would influence the masses. However, personal evolution is personal, and the primary aim is to improve oneself.

In addition, the road to personal evolution that a particular individual undertakes may not be applicable to another person. Our paths are unique because we are unique beings; we can be similar, but never identical. Otherwise, there would not be so many kinds of coffees or so many varieties of pizzas. Something that is a solution for one person would be a problem for someone else. Still, we all have to conform to certain societal norms and follow prescribed laws, which are specific to different parts of the world or countries.

This need to comply with rules does not mean that we should lose our individuality, even though we are daily bombard with advertisements that aim to put us all at the same level. Each being is individual with its characteristics, which must be recognized, known, and understood. From there, we can work to develop our personal skills to the maximum level possible, and find ways to minimize or eliminate our shortcomings. This process is define as evolution.

There are countless cases of people who have had near-death experiences that consequently, took a completely different attitude towards everything that surrounded them, in relation to material possessions, family, work, and so on. They completely changed their approach to life and their view of things. It is as if they found themselves. You could say that they finally integrated with their essence. The question is whether you have to go through such a dramatic experience to "reset" the system to start looking at things from another perspective.

We can examine this idea via a mental exercise, whereby we would imagine what would society look like, if each of its members worked first on itself for improving and stop comparing its life with that of others to see where they fit in the value scale. What would happen if we all stopped justifying our problems because others also have them, so that we do not have to do anything to fix them? What would it take us to stop blaming somebody else for our circumstances or actions?

We have grown up with the wrong concept that we are well if we are in a better condition than the others, when the is that truth an evolved human being, is well with itself regardless of the circumstances of others.

Astrology is one of the things that has served me in my evolutionary journey and I can say that, after much learning and work done, I can see the results. One realizes, because it changes the perspective of things. Moreover, it changes ones perspective; it is not that the "outside" changed.

Astrology allows us to measure at what moment one is under the effect of a transit that could be an illusion and would make things look all well beyond it really is. Conversely, when the periods are complicated, where you see everything dark and bad, astrology gives you the information so the person can act to overcome such influences. Astrology also provides checkpoints that allow seeing in what evolutionary state a particular person is.

There are elements within our reach to help us cope with heavy or complicated transits. Meditation and other personal techniques are important, but they can be complicated to perform because of external factors, precisely in the moments that one needs it more. There are Binaural sounds, for example, that can be use instead, with beneficial results. A 30–60 minute session is enough to "unload" an emotional load, a complicated day and so on, and it can be done at any time, even in bed before going to sleep.

There are police departments in the United States that use these techniques with their agents at the end of their shift and before returning home. This allows them to relax, lower the tension, put aside the problems of the workday, and not carry that entire burden home.

However, it is important to emphasize that you cannot live a crazy life and then use alternative methods to try to pass through the complicated moments. In some cases, the way of life must change if things do not go as one wants. Alternative methods are helpful, but are in no way the solutions.

As we can see, there are ways to minimize the burden generated by heavy planetary transits. Negative energies accumulate in a similar way to how debts accumulate, one on top of the other and with interest. When we act under pressure or in difficult situations, many factors of our personality and characteristics come into play. We already talked about the programming that we suffer, which is compounded by the aspects of our natal chart. In the face of a heavy planetary transit, each person can respond in two ways—towards the outside world or towards the inside.

Outwardly, we define it as an energy discharge (low vibration/negative) which, by its nature, will generate more of the same. When the response is inward, that negative energy is being concentrated in the intervening organ or organs, depending on the signs that the aspected houses/planets meet.

It is impossible for a release of negative energy, both internally and externally, to generate positive outcomes.

At this point it is worth remembering that negative energies, which are of low vibration, are recognized in the human body as a disease, and the cells that make up the corresponding organs will lower their electrical activity, as described in the part about the human body.

Not everything is black or white, but rather is some shade of gray. Within this grayscale spectrum, a reaction to the outside world, besides ventilating bad energy, could also have an impact on the body. For example, a square of Saturn and Mars could be represented by breaking a bone because of an action. Still, as managing our moods is the key to everything, all efforts should be focused on that aspect.

If you recall, all cells carry a charge, the level of which depends on the environment. We can explore these concepts further using analogy, whereby instead of talking about ADPs and ATPs, we will refer to money.

Let us say that a certain job generates X amount of money. With that money, I can afford my house, my car, and other material possessions. However, if my income depends on sales (the environment), if the sales decline, I will have less money to pay for my house, my car, and other expenses. The creditors will arrive, and will take everything I have, rendering me destitute and homeless.

Is there a difference in the way things work? Looks like a similar process. We are dependent both on our abilities to perform a job (birth chart), and the environment that surrounds us due to events that can harm sales (planetary transits) and the consequences that this may have on us (result). In this evaluation, you cannot leave history aside. If you saved money when you had enough, the decrease in income will affect you, but not to the point of losing your belongings to the creditors.

Today depends on yesterday. This applies to everything around us, including ourselves.

We could define this as the "mechanical" part of everything. However, as "human beings," we are much more than machines. Not only do we have our free will, but we have the capacity for using all the parts of our complex system that is the human body, which has an immense potential for development, with the possibility of managing our energies and, therefore, with the ability to level the imbalances in our environment. In addition, if by now it is still not yet clear, we can use our free will to overcome most external circumstances. Monks meditating to the inclemency with freezing temperatures, with snow falling on them, yet they do not freeze, can best exemplify this. Does anyone have any doubt that the monks are generating their own energy to compensate for the cold? They have the same organism as we do. However, unlike us, they have mastered the ability to control their "environment."

Planetary transits are classify as a part of the "environment." They would not be consider as something "external," but as a part of the functioning of things. Everything is interconnect with everything; we cannot disconnect astrology and the functioning of the planets from the rest.

For us, who are not as advanced as the monks are, finding ourselves involved in our daily routine, having to attend to our obligations, it may be hard to find the time to maintain the road map to evolution. This is why the understanding of the natal chart and the knowledge of planetary transits is fundamental.

If necessary, there are numerous elements and techniques we can adopt to help us in difficult periods. The goal is to become a better being tomorrow than we are today.

Integration of technology and astrology with the purpose of incorporating millennial knowledge is necessary, as it would help us reach the new generations who already manage technology in a natural way, but who do not know the base and wisdom of astrology.

This could compare to what happened to the development of astrology with the integration of astrology and psychology that Rudhyar did, which is the most recent upgrade that astrology had.

www.elnuevocamino.com[1]

---

1. http://www.elnuevocamino.com

About the Author

Edu Petriati, a computer scientist and astrologer, introduced a new look at astrology in 2018 with the book Astrology in the 21st Century, which was followed by Astrology in the 21st Century – Evolution. His extensive career in the technological sector and after years of studying and practicing astrology, he presents this book as a proposal seeking to delve into the reason for life, before and after passing through this plane and seeing the purpose behind the things.

Read more at https://www.elnuevocamino.com.